The APACHES

People of the Southwest

JENNIFER FLEISCHNER

NATIVE AMERICANS
THE MILLBROOK PRESS
BROOKFIELD, CONNECTICUT

The author would like to thank Judith A. Brundin,
Education Supervisory Specialist, National Museum
of the American Indian, Smithsonian Institution,
for her careful reading of the manuscript and her
many helpful comments and suggestions.

Cover: "Apache Family," 1938, by Allan Houser, Chiricahua
Apache. Photography courtesy of the Fred Jones Jr. Museum
of Art at The University of Oklahoma.
Photographs courtesy of The Greenwich Workshop, Inc., Trumbull,
Conn. 06611: pp. 8—"The Savage Taunt" by Frank McCarthy © 1984,
The Greenwich Workshop, Inc., 12—"Search for the Renegades" by
Howard Terpning © 1982, The Greenwich Workshop, Inc.; Arizona
Historical Society: pp. 10–11, 26, 27, 49, 51; Bettmann Archive:
pp. 16, 41, 42; Wide World: p. 18; American Museum of Natural
History: pp. 20, 23, 29; Mead Publishing: pp. 32, 35, 55; The
Gilcrease Museum, Tulas: p. 44 ("California Crossing, South
Platte River," William H. Jackson, 1867); The Gerald Peters
Gallery, Santa Fe, N.M.: p. 47; Theodore Roosevelt Collection,
Harvard College Library: p. 52. Map by Joe Le Monnier

Library of Congress Cataloging-in-Publication Data
Fleischner, Jennifer.
The Apaches : people of the southwest / by Jennifer Fleischner.
p.   cm. —(Native Americans)
Includes bibliographical references and index.
Summary: Presents the history and culture of the Apaches.
ISBN 1-56294-464-9 (lib. bdg.)
1. Apache Indians—Juvenile literature.   [1. Apache Indians.
2. Indians of North America.]   I. Title.   II. Series.
E99.A6F53 1994 973'.04972—dc20 94-8315 CIP   AC

Published by The Millbrook Press
2 Old New Milford Road, Brookfield, Connecticut 06804

CONTENTS

The Apaches

APACHE LANDS

FACTS ABOUT
THE TRADITIONAL APACHE
WAY OF LIFE

GROUP NAME:
Apache

MAJOR BANDS:
Western, Chiricahua, Jicarilla, Kiowa-Apache, Lipan,
Mescalero, Mimbreno, Tonto, White Mountain

GEOGRAPHIC REGION:
New Mexico, Arizona, Texas,
Oklahoma, Colorado, Mexico

LANGUAGE FAMILY:
Anthapascan

HOUSE TYPE:
Tepees and wickiups (round brush huts)

MAIN FOODS:
Corn, beans, pumpkins, squash, dried meat,
fruits, nuts, wild plants (yucca and mescal)

*A contemporary artist captures the strength and defiance
of the Apache warriors in the Chiricahua Mountains.*

Chapter One

A FINAL SURRENDER

Kanseah crouched low behind a jagged rock, holding his field glasses steadily to his eyes. The small, thin boy had promised his uncle Geronimo that he would watch carefully for any movement in the valley below. It was August 23, 1886, and the tiny band of Chiricahua Apaches led by Geronimo and Nachise, son of Cochise — perhaps no more than fifty warriors, women, and children — had been hiding in the Mexican mountains for five months now. Hunger and fear were wearing them down. During their escape they had stolen cattle for food, but they had sometimes suffered for days without water. The U.S. soldiers had discovered their camp, and the Apaches skirmished with them every day. Soldiers had seized most of the Apaches' store of dried meats and scared away their horses. Afraid of being captured, the Apaches could not even hunt or gather food.

As young Kanseah huddled behind the rocks, he suddenly saw two dark spots moving toward him on the trail. Focusing carefully, he soon recognized the two as Apache scouts — they

were Martine and Kayihtah. Kanseah knew them both, for Kayihtah's cousin was in hiding with them, and Martine had trained to be a warrior with Geronimo's close friend Juh. Maybe they were bringing help!

As Martine and Kayihtah drew near, carrying a flour sack tied to a pole as a white flag, Kanseah scrambled back along the rocks to find Geronimo. As soon as he heard, the Apache leader called his warriors to a council. When they had gathered in a

A small band of Apaches, led by Geronimo (center) and Nachise (mounted on the horse next to Geronimo), poses for a photographer in the Mexican mountains in the late 1800s.

circle, Geronimo spoke bluntly. "It does not matter who they are. If they come closer they are to be shot." His dark eyes flashed with anger. But Yahnozha, his brother-in-law, protested, "They are our brothers. Let's find out why they come." The men argued while Kanseah listened respectfully. He wanted to be brave and fight, but an empty stomach was gnawing at his courage. Finally, Geronimo gave way, and the two scouts were allowed to enter the camp.

*The army used Apache scouts to pursue
Geronimo, sending them ahead to search
the mountain camps, as shown in this
contemporary painting, "Search for the
Renegades" by Howard Terpning.*

The message the Chiricahua Apaches were given that fateful day was simple: Surrender or be killed. Kayihtah looked sorrowful as he spoke to his family and friends. You are surrounded, he reminded them. Choose to stay here, and you will have no peace. "If you are awake at night and a rock rolls down the mountain or a stick breaks, you will be running. You even eat your meals running. You have no friends whatever in the world."

What could Geronimo do? Five thousand United States soldiers — one fourth of the entire army — surrounded the tiny band. The Apaches were exhausted from fear and hunger. How could Geronimo be sure they would not be killed as soon as they came out of hiding? Could he trust General Nelson A. Miles, the new commander in charge? If it had been up to Geronimo alone, perhaps he would have decided to hold out and fight. But according to tradition, Geronimo consulted his council, and they urged him to surrender.

The final surrender of Geronimo to General Miles took place on September 4, 1886, in Skeleton Canyon, on the border of Mexico and New Mexico, about 100 miles (160 kilometers) from Geronimo's birthplace. Geronimo rode down alone, unarmed, out of the mountains into the army camp. He got off his horse, approached the general, and waited silently and proudly for the conference to begin. The two men stood between the general's troopers on one side and Geronimo's warriors on the other. As described in his own account, General Miles spoke first, using an interpreter.

"General Miles is your friend," he said.

"I never saw him, but I have been in need of friends," Geronimo answered. "Why has he not been with me?" When this was translated, the soldiers burst out laughing. Geronimo waited to hear the terms of surrender. The Apaches would have to lay down their arms. No harm would come to them. And in five days, they and their families would be sent to a camp in Florida to live.

"This is what the President wants to do, get all of you together," Miles explained. Then he promised, "While I live you will not be arrested."

Geronimo did not completely trust the general. But he agreed to a treaty because he believed that President Grover Cleveland had specifically sent his word that he and his people should be unharmed. To cement their agreement, Geronimo and General Miles placed a large stone on a blanket before them. The peace between them, they said, was to last until this stone crumbled to dust. Then General Miles swept a spot of ground clear with his hand and said, "Your past deeds shall be wiped out like this and you will start a new life."

Early the next morning, Geronimo, Nachise, and three other Apache leaders rode with General Miles to Fort Bowie, 65 miles (105 kilometers) away. On the way, Geronimo gazed out at the familiar Chiricahua Mountains.

"This is the fourth time I have surrendered," he said.

"And I think it is the last time," answered Miles.

"THE PEOPLE" ▪ The road the Apaches traveled through history to Geronimo's fourth and final surrender dated back hundreds of years. They may have come down 1,000 to 700 years before from Canada, where they were part of an ancient Athapaskan-speaking language group. By the 1500s, the small family groups merged into different bands that were given names by the Spanish explorers: the Kiowa-Apaches, the Lipans, the Jicarillas, the Mescaleros, the Tontos, the Chiricahuas, the Mimbrenos, and the Western Apaches. The Apaches called themselves *N'de* or *Tinde*, from the word *tinneh*, meaning "the people." (The word "Apache" is from a Zuni word meaning enemy, and may have been used to name a group of warriors who took over an abandoned pueblo in northeastern Arizona called Navahu.) They controlled territories that ranged throughout the Southwest and the Plains, from southeastern Colorado to northern Mexico, across Arizona, New Mexico, Texas, and Oklahoma.

The Spanish explorers who came west in the 1530s and 1540s were the first white people the Apaches had ever seen. It is likely that the Apaches saw the Spaniards first; even in those days the Apaches hid in the hills to watch for intruders below.

Since the Apaches had no written language, there is no written record of what they thought of the Spaniards. But a Spaniard, Castaneda de Najera, who traveled with the explorer Francisco de Coronado, has left vivid descriptions of the people he met. According to Castaneda, the Apaches seemed to live completely on "cattle, for they neither plant nor harvest maize [corn]. With the skins they build their houses; with the skins they clothe and shoe themselves; from the skins they make ropes and also obtain wool. From the sinews they make thread,

Spaniard Francisco Coronado explored the American Southwest in the mid-1500s. For many Native Americans he and his men were the first Europeans they had ever seen.

with which they sew their clothing and likewise their tents. From the bones they shape awls, and the dung they use for firewood, since there is no other fuel in all that land."

These early encounters with the people from Europe changed the Apache way of life forever. For one thing, the Spaniards brought with them horses and guns, which the Apaches had never seen. Word of the marvelous power of these two wonders spread quickly among the Indians in Mexico and the Southwest. The Apaches quickly learned the value of horses, in part for food but mostly to ride while hunting. Eventually, they rode saddled horses into battle, carrying bows and arrows and guns.

The first of the many violent conflicts between the Apaches and the Spanish broke out in the 1590s, when the Spanish decided to colonize Apache territory. In the early summer of 1598, a powerful Spaniard named Don Juan de Oñate arrived in New Mexico with a vast army and a group of Catholic missionaries to establish a colony in what would be called New Spain. By 1610 the Spaniards had built their capital city, Sante Fe, with the help of the Pueblos. But the Apaches fought fiercely against the Spanish conquerors. They raided the Spanish settlements for cattle and supplies, using horses and guns that the Spaniards had introduced to them.

The century that followed was one of intensified, bloody conflicts between Apache warriors and Spanish colonizers and missionaries. During this time the Spanish were trying to make a new life for themselves in New Spain. But the Apaches were trying to defend their whole way of life.

*Apache territory was bordered on the west by the
rugged terrain of the Grand Canyon in Arizona.*

Chapter Two

APACHE LIFEWAYS

For most of the eighteenth and nineteenth centuries, the Apaches lived in family groups in camps — called *rancherias* by the Spanish — that could be moved easily. The rancherias consisted of tepees and the more temporary small, round brush huts called wickiups that were clustered together. It was usually the women who built the wickiups. To begin, they bent a circle of saplings, tying them at the center. Then they thatched the spaces between the poles with whatever they could find — yucca leaves, reeds from rivers, or grass. Leaving a smoke hole in the middle, the women then stretched a canvas around the outside. For the door they hung a skin or blanket flap. Working together, several women could build a wickiup in about four hours.

Each rancheria was self-sufficient. Farming was difficult in the hot, dry climate where often barely 10 inches (25.4 centimeters) of rain fell a year. Much of the land was pebble desert, cut across by canyons and mountainous ranges. However, some

To build a wickiup, the Apaches constructed a frame of saplings and then tied reeds, grass, or leaves to the poles. The final step was to wrap the wickiup in canvas to keep out wind, rain, and snow.

Apaches did grow corn, beans, pumpkins, and squash. When the cottonwood trees began to bloom, that was the time to put the seeds into the earth. In early days, before the reservation, the women did much of the planting, because the men were often away from home, hunting for food.

THE SEASONS ▪ Because the Apaches relied mostly on hunting and gathering, families moved several times a year to make sure they had plenty to eat. With the changing seasons, they followed the deer, bison, mountain sheep, antelope, rabbits, turkeys, quails, and pigeons that the men and boys hunted for food. Spring and fall were considered the best times for hunting. Also at regular times during the year, Apache families set out from their camps to gather wild plants, fruits, or nuts.

Today, we divide the year into four seasons: winter, spring, summer, and fall. Summer is often the time for vacation, and fall the time for school. But to the Apaches, the year was divided into six time periods, each a distinct time for gathering special wild foods.

In Little Eagles (early spring), the narrow-leaved yucca was plentiful. After baking the stalks, the women dried them so that they could be stored in caves for a year until they were eaten. Many Leaves (late spring and early summer) was the time to gather mescal, the most important plant in the Apache diet. Several women would leave for the hills for days at a time to gather the cabbage-sized heads. The stalks were cut and roasted or baked in a pit. Most of the mescal was dried in the sun and stored for later use. Part of the dried crown was sometimes mixed with juniper or sumac berries, piñon nuts or wal-

Roasting
Pumpkin Seeds

Pumpkins were probably one of the earliest crops planted by the Apaches. There were special songs, prayers, and lucky planters for them. Pumpkins were often boiled, mashed, and then stirred into boiling ground corn to be eaten as a pudding. Sometimes they were cut in thin slices and fried. Pumpkin seeds were eaten uncooked or after roasting.

Here is a recipe for roasting pumpkin seeds.

You will need:
  1 pumpkin
  A knife for slicing the pumpkin
  A large spoon for scooping out the seeds
  A flat pan in which to cook the pumpkin seeds
  Salt

With help from an adult, slice open the pumpkin. Scoop out the seeds, using the spoon and your hands. Remove pulp from the seeds and spread them out on the pan. Sprinkle seeds with a little salt. Place pan in the oven and roast the seeds lightly at 300° (may take 10 to 15 minutes). Using an oven mitt or potholder, remove the pan from the oven and turn off the oven. Let the seeds cool before eating.

nuts, and then eaten. Juice from the mescal was used for making liquor.

Fruit was ripe for picking during Large Leaves (midsummer). Beans, nuts, and seeds were the bounty of Thick with Fruit (late summer, early fall), Earth Reddish Brown (late fall), and even Ghost Face (winter). Honey could be gotten all year round. When the women gathered yucca stalks, they looked out for the hives that sometimes were tucked in the stalks. Boys who found a hive swarming with angry bees would pretend to be fighting a battle with the enemy. They were stung often, but by continuing to fight (sometimes with an audience of adults) the boys proved their bravery as young warriors.

The "Apache Reaper," by the famous nineteenth-century photographer Edward Curtis.

Summer food-gathering journeys, which would last from ten days to a month, were an annual ritual. During the summer, when the corn was about 3 feet (1 meter) high, entire families, sometimes joined by neighbors, would set off to collect wild plants and fruits.

The women usually organized these food-gathering trips. (Except for harvesting mescal, men rarely gathered food — although boys and girls sometimes gathered seeds together when they were courting.) The women loaded all of their family's belongings onto a few horses. Although they left behind the large grindstone, called the *metate*, they packed the *mano*, a flat stone used to grind dried foods. They also took digging sticks, poles to knock fruit or nuts off the trees, cactus tongs, knives, carrying baskets, and sacks.

Traveling slowly across the mountains and hills, the men went first to protect the family, then came the women and, lastly, the children. Whatever supplies had not fit on the horses, the women hauled as they walked along. Sometimes the small children rode the horses; other times they walked. The boys carried the torches for making fire. Crossing rivers swollen by floods could be an adventure. So that they wouldn't fall off, all of the children were tied together by a yucca-fiber rope on a single horse. The men pulled the women across with two ropes tied around their waists. The strongest ropes were made of rawhide. Sometimes, though, several people crossed by grabbing onto the tails of their horses.

The Apaches, like other Indian groups, believed that if they left their camp exactly as it was when they lived there, they would be affected by what happened there while they were away. So to avoid bad luck, before the family left to move to the next place they would smooth over the fire pit and pile the beds made of weeds and grass into the center. Unfortunately, if a bear or some other animal considered to have dark powers came into the old camp and left its droppings, the family would be sure to have something go wrong soon.

CHILDHOOD ▪ Children were very special to Apache families. As soon as a baby was born, the midwife blessed it in a special washing ceremony. She bathed the infant in lukewarm water mixed with her saliva, then dried it with grass and wrapped it in a soft blanket. She also might sprinkle the baby with plant pollen, which was considered sacred, or scatter fire ashes in the four directions. To the Apaches, the directions — east, north, south, and west — stood for power.

Apache names were meant to reflect something special about the person. Baby names were only the first names the Apaches used, and they usually did not keep them beyond childhood. Geronimo's baby name was Go-yath-khla, which means Sleepy or Yawns. "Geronimo," the name we know him by, was given to him by the Mexicans, who called on Saint Jerome for protection whenever he charged, "*Cuidado!* Watch out! *Geronimo!*"

Babies were strapped tight and carried on their mothers' backs in a cradleboard, made of an oak frame covered with buckskin. Like mothers today who hang toys from their children's cribs, Apache mothers hung small feathers, pinecones, beads, or a squirrel's tail from the top of the cradleboard for the child to look at.

A little group of Mescalero Apache children poses solemnly for the camera. Apache children tended to be serious; even the games they played mimicked skills, such as hunting, that they would use as adults.

Two important childhood ceremonies launched the Apache child in life. These were the first haircut and the fitting of the first pair of moccasins. The medicine man or woman, called a *di-yin*, performed both rituals. In the spring after the child outgrew the cradleboard, the di-yin cut the child's hair very short, except for a few long strands. After childhood, haircuts were thought to bring bad luck, so adults rarely cut their hair.

A medicine man, like the one shown here, would perform the rituals of the first haircut and the fitting of the first pair of moccasins for Apache children.

The moccasin ceremony took place when an Apache child was two years old. At this time, children were led through their first ceremonial steps—four steps in each direction for good fortune. Then adults and children exchanged gifts and celebrated until dark.

As they grew up, children were taught to share, to be kind, to not steal or play tricks, to have good manners, and to respect adults. Also, because a noisy baby or child might give away the location of their camp to an enemy, children were taught to value silence. This is also why Apaches rarely kept dogs as pets; loud barking might lead the enemy right to their camps.

Boys and girls were taught by their elders the skills they would need to be productive and resourceful adults. Apaches believed that children should learn through observation and experience, not by being sat down and told what to do.

LESSONS FOR BOYS ▪ Apache boys had no books on how to hunt. Instead, fathers and older warriors showed young boys how to shoot with a bow and arrow, the most important hunting weapon used by the Apaches. At the age of eight, when he was old enough to leave the camp alone, an Apache boy was expected to hunt small game for himself. It was a matter of pride to be a good shot.

When he was fifteen or sixteen, the Apache boy went on his first deer hunt with his father, uncles, and maternal grandfather. Deer hunting was an important part of the life of an Apache man, and special care was taken to teach boys to find favor with the special hunting powers.

Young Apache males were trained by their elders to hunt deer with bows and arrows.

From the older men, a boy learned what he needed to know to be successful in the hunt. He memorized the hunting prayers and songs: "Panther Boy, there is food in your camp. Hurry and bring me the forked-horn deer that you raise." He was taught to look for favorable signs. For example, an owl hooting near the camp would mean that many deer would appear in the morning. He was instructed not to show confidence before a hunt, or take out his basket to bring meat home, or eat before leaving for the hunt. Such behavior might spoil the hunt, since the special powers took pity on hunters who were hungry and humble.

To get close to a deer, a hunter might wear a deer mask. Made of the stuffed head of a deer, the mask covered the hunter's head entirely. If he approached from downwind, a good hunter could get within a few feet of an unsuspecting deer. A skillful stalker could even call a doe by imitating the bleating of a fawn, which he did by blowing across a leaf held horizontally between his lips.

Boys were also trained to be warriors. As part of his passage to manhood, an Apache boy had to master the rules of war and raiding. He had to be able to provide for and protect his family. As with hunting, there were many rules for waging war and raiding. For instance, "You should travel only at night across the open places. You can travel during the day in the mountains if you want, but if you cross a desert by day the soldiers or Mexicans would see you and catch you." Or another rule, "If it is a hot day and you want to rest, lie up in brush or grass. Never go to cool shade, no matter what. If there are soldiers around, that is where they will be and you will walk right into them."

LESSONS FOR GIRLS ▪ Because girls and young women had to be able to guard the camp while the men were away, they were also taught to take care of horses, and to use rifles, knives, and bows to fight and to hunt small game. While boys were training to be hunters and warriors, girls were taught about food gathering, cooking, tanning deer hides, sewing, and basket weaving. These chores were as necessary to the survival of the people as were hunting and raiding. In fact, it was thought that women could survive for a long time without aid from men, but men could not live long without the help of women.

Girls learned how to identify plants and how to shell, hull, husk, and strip the plants to find the parts that were good to eat. They learned to dry corn by removing just enough of the outer husk, placing a pile of corncobs on the fire, and removing them from the flames at just the right moment.

When men brought the skins of animals home, women and girls soaked them in water overnight, then scraped and pulled off the hair. After this, they hung the skin over a post to scrape it clean of fat and meat. Finally, after more soaking and scraping, women and girls sewed moccasins, headdresses decorated with feathers, leggings, bags, blankets, dresses, and shirts. They could dye these using extracts from boiled roots (yellows), tree barks and berries (reds), and walnut juice (browns).

Girls also learned how to cook the best part of the venison rare by placing it directly on the coals or on a spit held over the fire. One favorite recipe involved boiling and chopping up venison with acorn meal. Apache girls and women could also bake meat in a pit covered with wet grass. This pit was an Apache oven.

A young Apache girl dances in her coming-of-age costume. Once the ceremony is completed, the girl is considered to be a woman and ready for marriage.

For girls, the most meaningful event other than marriage was the coming-of-age ceremony called *Nah-ih-es*. This four-day ceremony celebrated a young girl's entry into womanhood. It was the most important ceremony in Apache tradition. Some families began preparations a year in advance. They preserved extra food and the five extra buckskins it took to make the puberty costume.

The ceremony began at dawn on the first day when, as the girl faced east, an older woman marked the girl's nose with pollen. (This ritual was repeated over and over throughout the ceremony.) Then the girl was dressed in the coming-of-age costume. This costume was elaborately decorated and painted with a crescent moon, morning star, rainbow, and sunbeams. From that moment on, the girl was thought to have the power to bless the Apaches by giving birth to new people.

For the next four days the girl stayed in a tepee specially built for the occasion, and the solemn ritual continued. The older woman attendant said prayers for the girl, and a singer, usually a man, sang songs meant to guide the girl toward a long, successful life. A di-yin chose the dancers who entertained the guests and spread good luck.

The ceremony ended with a feast and an exchange of gifts. The girl was now ready for marriage.

ADULTHOOD ▪ Boys and girls played together until they were in their teens, when play gave way to serious courtship. Like teenagers everywhere, Apache boys and girls were often awkward and shy about showing their feelings at first. But, as soon as they decided to marry, their families took over the marriage arrangements. The Apaches are matrilineal (they trace their descent through the wife's family) and matrilocal, which means that newlyweds moved to the camp of the wife's family.

Most Apache men had only one wife at a time, although they were allowed to have several wives at once. Some believe this became necessary in the 1800s, when so many men were killed in wars against Mexicans and U.S. troopers that women far outnumbered men. Sometimes the wives all lived in the same wickiup, but more often each wife had her own. It is said that Geronimo had at least three wives, although not all at once. An unhappily married Apache could get a divorce by simply moving out of the camp.

APACHE VALUES AND BELIEFS ▪ Both boys and girls were taught Apache values through Coyote stories. Coyote was a trickster who did many silly and wicked things, but always received his proper punishment. One popular story told of how Coyote wanted to make his children spotted like two newly born fawns that he thought were pretty. "I want my children to look like that. How did you do it?" he asked their mother, the doe. She told him to put them in a cleft in the rocks, cover them with juniper, and set it on fire. When Coyote did this, the fire just burned the little coyotes. Some say this story was told to show how foolish Coyote was for wanting his babies to be what they weren't.

In addition to Coyote stories, the Apaches told about Yusn Life-giver, White-painted Woman, Killer of Enemies, and Child of the Water. These were the holiest spirits, who were there at the beginning of all things and set examples for Apaches.

When Yusn put Apaches on the earth, he instructed them to follow the holy way—the Apache values of generosity, kindness, and respect. But the Apaches could not follow Yusn's directions to be good for long. So down from the sacred mountains Yusn sent magical beings called *Ganhs* to help the Apaches on their journey through life. The Ganhs wore beautiful buckskin kilts and elaborate hooded headdresses and showed the Apaches how to cure sicknesses and pray for blessings. Even today, certain Apaches put on the costume of the Ganh and perform the intricate dance steps that help the sick or bless a girl during her coming-of-age ceremony.

Apache dancers costumed to represent the spirits called
Ganhs, performed to cure sickness and pray for blessings.

The Apaches also believed that everything in the world has a purpose and that all things are inhabited by a power for good or bad. An old Apache lesson teaches that "each thing in the world—the animals, the plants, the sky and stars and lightning—has a power behind it that makes it do what it does. What you can see is only a little of the whole thing. The power is in the spirit part. Some people can learn to reach the spirit part of something, and they become its di-yin. There is power in everything!"

Pollen from tule, piñon, oak, pine, sunflower, or corn was used in ceremonies because pollen was considered a good power. The four directions were good powers, too. The fearful powers were snakes, bears, crows, and lightning. Contact with any of these was sure to bring on sickness or other misfortunes, such as losing your teeth or going mad.

RECREATION ▪ The Apaches also loved to have fun. When they wanted to give a party or a social dance, the Apaches would brew a form of beer, called *tizwin*. At the Wheel Dance, single women chose their dance partners. Storytelling gatherings that lasted all night were also ways to spend time with friends. An old man or woman who was a skilled storyteller could keep an audience awake with tales of Coyote's misadventures.

Gambling was also a favorite pastime, and the Apaches bet on most of the games and sports that they played. Arrow-shooting contests, marble games, and wrestling were popular among men and boys. Women and men competed in foot and horseback races. The Chiricahua Apaches, Geronimo's band, loved a rough team sport called shinny. It was like soccer and

The Moccasin Game

According to Apache legends, the moccasin game was played between the animals and the birds when the earth was new. The Apaches play this game only in the winter, and often at night around a campfire.

Materials:
- a blanket
- 8 small bags (4 per team)
- 2 sticks, 2 feet (61 centimeters) long (1 per team)
- 1 small rounded object, such as a pebble, for hiding (the Apaches use a bone)
- 68 slips of paper for counters (the apaches use yucca leaves)

The counters are valued as follows:
- 64 are plain and worth 1 point each
- 4 are marked and worth 10 points each

The first team hides the pebble in one of its four bags, using the blanket to hide the bags until ready. A player from the other team uses the stick to strike the bag believed to hide the pebble. If he guesses right, his team wins the pebble and can take a turn hiding it. If the striker misses the bag by one on either side, the hiding team is awarded four counters, or points. If he misses by two or more, the hiders get ten points. The hiding team hides the pebble as long as the striker keeps missing. Players try to confuse the striker by singing and making noise. When the pile of counters is gone, each team pays the other from its own winnings.

hockey, but it did not have penalties, fouls, or time periods. The most important game for the men was the hoop-and-pole game, in which you had to catch a rolling hoop on a pole. Women were forbidden to even come near the hoop-and-pole field. Instead, they played a game called stave, which was played like a board game made on the ground with stones for markers and pieces.

As strong as the Apache culture was, it was no match for the furious struggle facing these Native Americans, as more and more strangers arrived in the Southwest, set on claiming Apache territory for their own.

Chapter Three

FIGHTING FOR THE LAND

The Apaches had lived and hunted for years across the Southwest. So when first the Spanish colonizers, then the Mexicans, and then the Americans, wanted their land, conflicts between the Apaches and the new arrivals flared. Misunderstanding, mistrust, or the settlers' greed for more land and wealth inevitably erupted into betrayal and battle.

By the time of the American Revolutionary War, the Apaches had a well-earned reputation as ferocious warriors. To discourage new Spanish settlements, they regularly raided the Spaniards' supplies and camps. The Apaches often took women captives, and seized food, horses, cattle, and guns.

To the Apaches, these attacks were acts of revenge. Some Spaniards had tried to subdue the Apaches peacefully. Bernardo de Galvez, who became viceroy of Mexico in 1786, thought that if the Spanish gave them gifts, food, and alcohol, the Apaches would grow dependent on the Spanish and not fight back. Church missionaries tried to manage the Apaches by converting Apache people to Roman Catholicism.

But many colonizers only wanted to destroy the Indians who inhabited the territory they wanted for themselves. Spanish horsemen frequently attacked Apache camps. They ruthlessly captured Apache men, women, and children to make them slaves in the mines and homes of wealthy Spanish and Mexican families. These bounty hunters could also make good money by selling Apache scalps. An Apache warrior's scalp could fetch a hundred dollars in the provinces, while a woman's was worth fifty dollars and a child's, twenty-five dollars.

Soon, the Apaches were fighting another enemy—the Americans. The Apaches' conflicts with the United States started to heat up in 1846, when Mexico and the United States went to war over Texas. Texas, a Mexican territory until it became independent in 1836, had been admitted into the union in 1845. Now Mexico wanted it back. The fighting lasted two years, until Mexico surrendered in 1848. Under the Treaty of Guadalupe-Hidalgo, Mexico turned over to the United States 500,000 square miles (1,295,000 square kilometers) of territory that included the northern parts of New Mexico and Arizona. More Apache territory was added five years later, when the United States bought from Mexico a 45,000-square-mile (116,550-square-kilometer) strip of southern New Mexico and Arizona. The U.S. government planned to build a railroad across Apache land to open a southern route to the West.

The 1848 treaty also stated that the United States would help to prevent Indians living in these territories from raiding settlements in Mexico. The Americans agreed to punish the

The Mexican War ended with Mexico turning over to the United States thousands of acres of land in New Mexico and Arizona that included important Apache territory. This Currier & Ives lithograph depicts the Battle of Mill el Rey in 1847, one year before the war ended.

raiders and to pay back Mexicans for their losses. This set the United States directly against the Apaches, for whom raiding had become a way of life.

MANIFEST DESTINY ▪ During the 1840s, Americans believed that it was their God-given right to take over the continent from coast to coast. The phrase "manifest destiny," coined by a newspaper editor in 1845, justified the country's urge to expand the nation's borders to take in Texas, Oregon, New Mex-

A painting by the famous western artist Charles M. Russell shows prospectors panning for gold in a desert stream.

ico, and California. Between the 1840s and the 1870s, thousands of miners, cattlemen, and settlers flocked west to the new territories. When gold was discovered in California in 1848, Americans and Europeans raced to the coast, frantic for riches. Soon prospective homesteaders were told that land in the Southwest was theirs for the taking. The Homestead Act of 1862 promised 160 acres (65 hectares) to anyone willing to farm them. Fighting between the Apaches and Americans intensified when gold was discovered in Tonto Apache territory in 1863.

Many of the pioneers flooding the Apaches' hunting ground did not want to listen to the Indians' claims to the land. All across the West, Indians defended their ancestral grounds in open warfare, ambushes, and raids. They also took revenge on settlers who mistreated them. The United States sent its army to protect the pioneers and to punish the Indians. The Apaches fought especially hard against the whites they called "white-eyed enemies," who swept across their land. But the 6,000 to 8,000 Apaches who were left by the mid-nineteenth century had little hope of fighting off the entire U.S. Army.

THE REVENGE OF MANGAS ▪ During the 1850s the United States built many forts throughout Apache territory. Soldiers were stationed at them to police Apache activities. New gold-mining sites were also dug throughout Apache territory. At this time, the most imposing Apache leader was Mangas Coloradas (Spanish for "Red Sleeves"). A huge man, Mangas was also intelligent and clever. He led the Warm Springs Apaches, who called themselves the *Tci-he-ende*, or "Red-paint People," after the color of their war paint. But unlike many Apache leaders, Mangas was influential in directing other Apache bands as well.

During the 1840s and 1850s, Mangas had friendly relations with Americans, as he directed raids primarily against Mexicans living along Mexico's northern border. But by 1860, Mangas was at war with the Americans because of an incident that had occurred at one of the mines near his territory. Mangas had gone to the miners' camps to ask the men to move south of the border to Sonora, where the land was much richer. Suspecting a trick, the miners tied Mangas to a post and

*The Apaches weren't the only Native Americans
caught up in the gold rush. Here, settlers cross
Sioux territory on their way west across the plains.*

whipped him until he could barely walk. As he staggered away, they jeered and hooted after him.

Mangas vowed revenge, and he began a rampage against the Americans. Mangas's Apaches attacked mail carriages and robbed a federal wagon train. They murdered nearly everyone aboard and killed the soldiers who were sent to escort them. It was not until 1863, when he was in his sixties, that Mangas was finally stopped. After persuading him to come to an army camp to discuss plans for peace, U.S. soldiers seized and arrested the great warrior while he slept. Guards burned his feet and legs with heated bayonets, then they shot him when he tried to flee. Before dumping his body in a shallow grave, they beheaded him.

THE WARRIOR COCHISE ▪ Brutality on the part of both sides persisted for many years. In 1860 a band of Apaches, probably Pinals, raided a settler's home, capturing a twelve-year-old boy. The boy's father ran to Fort Buchanan, where he told Lieutenant George Bascom that a group of Chiricahua Apaches, led by the famous warrior Cochise, held his son. Bascom sent a scouting party after the Indians, but they lost the trail. In January 1861, Bascom marched to Apache Pass in southeastern Arizona with fifty-four soldiers to make contact with Cochise. Cochise, a skilled fighter, appeared with six warriors, one of whom carried a white flag. Cochise met Bascom in his army tent and declared his innocence. But Bascom refused to believe him and tried to have him arrested. Pulling out a knife, Cochise made a slit in the tent and escaped. During his escape, his warriors were taken hostage.

But Cochise, who really *was* innocent, was not finished. The next day he returned with some warriors to a nearby stagecoach station where he was known. He captured the stationmaster and killed two other workers. That night, Cochise attacked the Overland Mail Coach, killing everyone but three drivers, whom he also took captive. Cochise and Bascom began negotiating to exchange their prisoners, but Bascom would not trade unless the twelve-year-old boy was returned. Before Cochise could get the boy from the Apaches who held him, two detachments of American soldiers filed into Apache Pass to find Cochise. Cochise probably believed that the Americans were determined to fight. The Apache leader escaped, but not before he had killed several American soldiers. Angered, the senior American officer, Captain Irwin, had Cochise's warriors executed. Three of them were related to Cochise. In revenge, Cochise killed more than 150 whites during the next two months. So began the Chiricahua's twenty-five-year war against the U.S. government.

MASSACRE AT CAMP GRANT ▪ During the war against the Apaches, it was said that no Americans were safe from the warrior's revenge. The Apaches suffered greatly, too. One of the worst episodes, the Camp Grant Massacre, took place on April 30, 1871. A mob of 148 Americans and Papago Indians from Tucson, who had had enough of Apache raiding, set upon several hundred sleeping Apaches who were living at Camp Grant in Arizona under the protection of Captain Frank Stanwood. About one hundred Apaches were killed, most of them women and children. Twenty-seven children were sold into slavery in

*In this painting by Frederic Remington, Geronimo
and his band are shown returning — apparently with
captured horses — from a raid into Mexico.*

Mexico or given to the Papagos. Only six were ever returned. Horrified, President Ulysses S. Grant demanded that the attackers be tried. Although charges were filed against 104 people, the jury took just nineteen minutes to find them all innocent.

GENERAL CROOK'S PLAN ▪ The Camp Grant Massacre took place when tension was increasing between Apaches and the U.S. government over Indian relocation. Beginning in the 1850s, the U.S. government had begun promising the Apaches that if they agreed to leave their hunting grounds, they would be given money and enough good land for their people to live on. These areas of land, called reservations, were to be set aside for the individual bands. Government officials planned reservations with the hope that they would bring about a peaceful solution to the fight over the land between the Indians and miners and settlers. The government also sent men to teach the Apaches how to farm, hoping this would put an end to Apache raiding.

By the 1870s it was clear that the government wanted to confine all of the Apache people to reservations. In 1871–1872, the United States created four Apache reservations in Arizona. In 1872, General George Crook, a veteran of many battles against the Indians, took charge of moving all the Apaches onto reservations.

Crook believed that Apache raiding and cruelty to whites arose out of necessity, because the desert did not provide them with much food. Still, he felt that he must first defeat the Apaches in battle before settling the Apache reservations. Using friendly Apaches as scouts and soldiers in his own army,

General George Crook was accompanied by Apache scouts when he rode into Apache territory with plans to force the Native Americans onto reservations.

Crook quickly conquered the western Apache band, the Tonto. Then, in 1874, the United States started a policy of "concentration." This meant that three Apache bands—the Western, Chiricahua, and Yavapai—would be moved to one reservation in San Carlos, Arizona.

To many of the Apaches, San Carlos was unbearable. Fights broke out among the different bands, who were not used to one another's ways. They disliked the feeling of imprisonment, and the soldiers and agency that watched over them. And being confined to a hot, humid place was hard for a people who for generations had lived and roamed freely in the mountains. One of Crook's lieutenants, Britton Davis, called the place "Hell's Forty Acres."

APACHE RESISTANCE ▪ Some Apaches actively resisted being forced to live on reservations. In 1877, Chief Victorio, leader of the Mimbrenos, fled into the mountains with about three hundred followers, eighty of whom stayed in the mountains with him. Heavy rains washed away their trail, and the cavalry could not track them. Victorio and this band of warriors led countless raids until 1880, when they were crushed at the two-day Battle of Tres Castillos in northern Mexico. More than half of the Mimbreno Apaches, including Victorio, were killed.

Meanwhile, the Chiricahua Apache Geronimo was fast becoming the subject of legends. By the 1880s, Geronimo had been leading raids against Mexican and American villages for twenty years. As conflict with the Indians grew, soldiers and settlers alike came to view the Apaches as the most ferocious of all Indians and Geronimo as the most ferocious of all Apaches.

Geronimo's life became a cycle of capture, surrender, and escape — a cycle that was repeated four times between 1876 and 1886. One famous incident occurred in early 1886, when Geronimo agreed to General George Crook's demand that he surrender, only to escape while being led to prison. The embarrassed U.S. Army replaced Crook with General Nelson Miles, and it was to him that Geronimo, the "human tiger," finally surrendered on September 4, 1886, at Skeleton Canyon.

Geronimo, before his final surrender.

*Geronimo (third from left) rode in President Theodore
Roosevelt's inaugural parade in 1907. By this time the
Apaches were considered thoroughly civilized.*

Chapter Four

APACHE
LIFE TODAY

When Geronimo surrendered to General Miles, peace did come to Gran Apacheria. Breaking their promise, the United States made all the Apaches prisoners of war and sent them far from their homeland to a camp in Florida. Later, the Apaches were moved to a camp in Alabama. Finally, they were transported to Fort Sill, Oklahoma.

During this period, reservation life practically destroyed Apache culture. Living at Fort Sill, Geronimo gave up being a medicine man to his people and became a national celebrity. He took advantage of the white people's fascination with Indians and sold tourists autographs, photographs, and buttons from his coat. In 1907 he was paid to ride in costume on horseback in the inaugural parade for President Theodore Roosevelt. This was meant to show that the government was "civilizing" the Indians.

Geronimo died in 1909, and instead of being buried in the Apaches' traditional burial grounds, he was buried among the graves of other Apache prisoners in the Fort Sill cemetery. In 1943 an elderly Apache told a reporter for the Fort Sill *Army News* that soon after his burial, Geronimo's body was taken by some of his former warriors and buried in a secret place away from the reservation. Although many denied this story, the Apache stood by his account of what would have been Geronimo's final escape.

In the 1970s and 1980s the United States supported a policy known as "self-determination." This meant that the federal government would work with local tribal governments to preserve their culture and rich heritage.

Today, many Apaches live on or near reservations in Arizona, New Mexico, and Oklahoma. But life for some Apache people on and off the reservation remains hard. Many Apaches earn their living by raising cattle, lumbering, sheepherding, and working in their successful tourist industry. However, unemployment remains high.

Above all, Apache people today are proud of their heritage. They are determined to pass their culture and traditions down to the next generation. The descendants of the great warriors and brave women still follow their ancestors' ways even as they live in modern American society.

The great-granddaughter of Cochise, Elbys Naiche Hugar, was an example of how today's Apaches combine the two cultures. Mrs. Hugar helped keep Apache traditions and language alive. She ran the Mescalero Apache Cultural Center in New Mexico, where she showed visitors photographs of famous Apache people, and displayed handmade Apache beadwork, jewelry, and moccasins. She coauthored the only Mescalero

*An Apache girl, attended by her friends and
family, receives instructions from her godmother
at the girl's coming-of-age ceremony.*

Apache dictionary. She taught her daughters to gather Indian foods in the fall and Indian medicines in May. Her coming-of-age ceremony was in 1944; her granddaughter's took place in 1990. As an old woman, Cochise's great-granddaughter explained how she felt about being an Indian: "Once you're an Indian, you're always an Indian. Maybe you can change your ways. Dress different. Dress like the modern ways and change your attitude to be more in the modern way. But you can also hang onto your culture if you really believe in the traditions. . . . If you don't practice your traditions, you're going to lose them. If you don't live like the old ways every once in a while, you're going to lose your culture."

AN APACHE STORY: HOW COYOTE STOLE FIRE

Back in the early times no one down here on the earth had fire. It was not allowed. The only beings on earth who had permission for fire were a camp of Firefly People high up on a bluff. The people down below were cold and had a hard time, and had to eat raw meat. They didn't know how to get up that bluff to get fire from the Firefly People.

One time Coyote was going around the base of that bluff and saw some of the Fly Little Boys playing the arrow game. He started to play with them, and pretty soon he won all their arrows from them. He said, "Listen, I have won all the arrows but you gave me a hard time for them, so I'm going to give you some back. In a while I'm going up the bluff there and tell your fathers how good you are. I will give the arrows to the boy that tells me about the trail."

The youngest Fly Little Boy was tricked into telling Coyote about the trail. When Coyote reached the camp of the Flies, he told them all their enemies were killed, and he wanted to celebrate.

Those Flies got a dance going and Coyote went off. He found a juniper tree and tied little strips of bark under his tail. Then he went back to the dance. "I am going to celebrate with you now," he said. In the middle of the dancers was a big fire. Coyote danced over to the fire and waved his tail in it.

One of the Flies saw him and said, "Hey, old man, you're going to catch your tail on fire!"

Coyote said, "No, I won't. This is just how I celebrate." He did that several more times.

Finally he left his tail in the fire long enough and it started to burn. Then all at once Coyote got out of that camp and ran away. The Flies all said, "There he goes! Get him! He got our fire from us!"

That Coyote ran hard, and his flaming tail set fire to everything along the way. Flies were chasing him and trying to put out the fires. Finally some of them flew away to find Wasp. They told him, "Make it rain, old man! Coyote has got our fire and is setting the world on fire. Hurry up!"

Wasp got up and made it rain. The rain started putting out all the fires, even the one on Coyote's tail.

Coyote saw it start to rain and he ran to where some bees had a hive in a sotol stalk. When he got there he had just a little fire left, under his tail, where it was scorched yellow. Coyotes still have this place, they say.

He got the bees to hide the fire in the stalk, and this is how we got fire. We still make our fire from sotol stalks, because the fire is in it.

Coyote got it for us, even though he nearly burned the world up doing it. He was a rough fellow, but he tried to help us out.

IMPORTANT DATES

1300s–1400s	Apaches migrate from Canada to southwestern United States
mid-1500s	Spanish explorers cross Apache territory
1600s–1700s	Apaches raid Spanish and Mexican settlements
1846	Mexican War begins
1848	Treaty of Guadalupe-Hidalgo
1849	At the height of the gold rush thousands of Americans and Europeans rush west
1850s	Construction of forts throughout Apache territory
1861	Cochise meets Lieutenant Bascom at Apache Pass; Apache wars begin
1862	Homestead Act
1871	Camp Grant Massacre
1871–1872	Four Apache reservations created in Arizona
1880	Victorio defeated at Tres Castillos
1886	Geronimo surrenders to General Miles at Skeleton Canyon
1968	American Indian Movement founded
1970s–1980s	U.S. government begins policy of "self-determination"

GLOSSARY

Athapaskan. An ancient people and the most widely scattered language group of Native Americans. Apaches are Athapaskan-speaking peoples living in American Southwest and Mexico.

di-yin. A person with supernatural powers who uses magic to interpret dreams and visions, cure the sick, and control events.

Gran Apacheria. Spanish term for Apache territory.

homesteaders. Settlers granted parcels of 160 acres (65 hectares) of public land by U.S. government.

maize. Indian corn.

metate. Grindstone.

N'de, Tinde. Names Apaches call themselves, from *tinneh*, a word in Apache dialect meaning "the people."

power. In Apache religion, a good and/or evil force that affects humans.

rancherias. Apache camps.

reservation. A tract of land set aside by treaty for the occupation and use of Indians.

sotol. A plant of the agave family that grows in the Southwest.

wickiups. Small, round brush huts used by southwestern Indians.

Yusn Life-giver. God of the sky who was believed to have created the universe.

BIBLIOGRAPHY

*for children

Ball, Eve. *In the Days of Victorio*. Tucson: University of Arizona Press, 1970.

Barrett, S.M. *Geronimo's Story of His Life*. Taken down and edited by S. M. Barrett. New York: Duffield & Company, 1906.

Buskirk, Winfred. *The Western Apache: Living With the Land Before 1950*. Norman, Okla.: University of Oklahoma Press, 1986.

Debo, Angie. *Geronimo: The Man, His Time, His Place*. Norman, Okla.: University of Oklahoma Press, 1976.

Haley, James L. *Apaches: A History and Culture Portrait*. Garden City, N.Y.: Doubleday & Company, 1981.

Kestler, Frances Roe, ed. *The Indian Captivity Narrative: A Woman's View*. New York: Garland Publishing, Inc, 1990.

*McCall, Barbara. *Apache*. New York: Chelsea House Publishers, 1990.

*Melody, Michael E. *The Apache*. New York: Chelsea House, 1988.

*Shorto, Russell. *Geronimo*. Morristown, N.J.: Silver Burdett, 1989.

Stockel, W. Henrietta. *Women of the Apache Nation: Voices of Truth*. Reno: University of Nevada Press, 1991.

Terrell, John Upton. *Apache Chronicle*. New York: World Publishing Co., 1972.

INDEX

Page numbers in *italics* refer to illustrations.